TO KILL A MOC...

by
Harper Lee

Student Packet

Written by
Mina Watts,
Gloria Levine, M.A.,
and Maureen Kirchhoefer, M.A.

Contains masters for:

2	Prereading Activities
7	Vocabulary Activities
1	Study Guide
4	Character Analysis Activities
3	Literary Analysis Activities
2	Comprehension Activities
1	Critical Thinking Activity
3	Quizzes
1	Novel Test

PLUS Detailed Answer Key

Teacher Note

Selected activities, quizzes, and test questions in this Novel Units® Student Packet are labeled with the appropriate reading/language arts skills for quick reference. These skills can be found above quiz/test questions or sections and in the activity headings.

Note

The 2010 Grand Central Publishing paperback edition of the novel, © 1960 by Harper Lee, was used to prepare this guide. The page references may differ in other editions. Novel ISBN: 978-0-446-31078-9

Please note: This novel deals with sensitive, mature issues. Parts may contain profanity, sexual references, and/or descriptions of violence. Please assess the appropriateness of this novel for the age level and maturity of your students prior to reading and discussing it with them.

To order, contact your local school supply store, or—

Novel Units, Inc.
P.O. Box 97
Bulverde, TX 78163-0097

Web site: novelunits.com

Note to the Teacher

Selected activities, quizzes, and test questions in this Novel Units® Student Packet are labeled with the following reading/language arts skills for quick reference. These skills can be found above quiz/test questions or sections and in the activity headings.

Basic Understanding: The student will demonstrate a basic understanding of written texts. The student will:
- use a text's structure or other sources to locate and recall information (Locate Information)
- determine main idea and identify relevant facts and details (Main Idea and Details)
- use prior knowledge and experience to comprehend and bring meaning to a text (Prior Knowledge)
- summarize major ideas in a text (Summarize Major Ideas)

Literary Elements: The student will apply knowledge of literary elements to understand written texts. The student will:
- analyze characters from a story (Character Analysis)
- analyze conflict and problem resolution (Conflict/Resolution)
- recognize and interpret literary devices (flashback, foreshadowing, symbolism, simile, metaphor, etc.) (Literary Devices)
- consider characters' points of view (Point of View)
- recognize and analyze a story's setting (Setting)
- understand and explain themes in a text (Theme)

Analyze Written Texts: The student will use a variety of strategies to analyze written texts. The student will:
- identify the author's purpose (Author's Purpose)
- identify cause and effect relationships in a text (Cause/Effect)
- identify characteristics representative of a given genre (Genre)
- interpret information given in a text (Interpret Text)
- make and verify predictions with information from a text (Predictions)
- sequence events in chronological order (Sequencing)
- identify and use multiple text formats (Text Format)
- follow written directions and write directions for others to follow (Follow/Write Directions)

Critical Thinking: The student will apply critical-thinking skills to analyze written texts. The student will:
- write and complete analogies (Analogies)
- find similarities and differences throughout a text (Compare/Contrast)
- draw conclusions from information given (Drawing Conclusions)
- make and explain inferences (Inferences)
- respond to texts by making connections and observations (Making Connections)
- recognize and identify the mood of a text (Mood)
- recognize an author's style and how it affects a text (Style)
- support responses by referring to relevant aspects of a text (Support Responses)
- recognize and identify the author's tone (Tone)
- write to entertain, such as through humorous poetry or short stories (Write to Entertain)
- write to express ideas (Write to Express)
- write to inform (Write to Inform)
- write to persuade (Write to Persuade)
- demonstrate understanding by creating visual images based on text descriptions (Visualizing)
- practice math skills as they relate to a text (Math Skills)

Name _____

Anticipation and Reaction

Directions: Consider the following statements before you read the novel. Place a checkmark in one of the boxes to show whether you agree or disagree with each statement, and provide your reasoning. After you have completed the novel, mark your response again. Provide an explanation if your opinion has changed.

Statement	Response Before Reading	Response After Reading
1. Adults are braver than children.	☐ you agree with the statement ☐ you disagree with the statement	☐ you agree with the statement ☐ you disagree with the statement
2. Kindness is key to having a strong character.	☐ you agree with the statement ☐ you disagree with the statement	☐ you agree with the statement ☐ you disagree with the statement
3. The potential for evil is inside every person.	☐ you agree with the statement ☐ you disagree with the statement	☐ you agree with the statement ☐ you disagree with the statement
4. The lessons a person learns in youth can be useful for a lifetime.	☐ you agree with the statement ☐ you disagree with the statement	☐ you agree with the statement ☐ you disagree with the statement

What Do You See Coming?

Directions: Before you begin reading, look at the following parts of the novel. Based on each part of the novel listed, make a prediction. Write your predictions in the boxes provided.

1. Front Cover	2. Epigraph	3. First Page	4. Back Cover
?	?	The whole story will be a flashback on the things that led up to the event of Jem breaking his arm.	There is going to be alot of mixed emotions. On the back is says that the book experiences love, hatred, kindness, cuelty ...

Name _____

Vocabulary Multiple Choice

assuaged	dictum	taciturn	unsullied
vapid	malevolent	predilection	nebulous
indigenous	sojourn	iniquities	contentious
monosyllabic	fractious	disapprobation	

Directions: Choose the word or phrase closest in meaning to the bolded vocabulary word.

1. **assuaged**   relieved   deterred   confirmed

2. **dictum**   warning   statement   obligation

3. **taciturn**   reserved   dull   compliant

4. **unsullied**   uninvoked   unspoiled   unmatched

5. **vapid**   overdone   altered   bland

6. **malevolent**   alleged   wicked   invisible

7. **predilection**   preference   evaluation   pronouncement

8. **nebulous**   recurrent   prominent   vague

9. **indigenous**   rumored   native   renowned

10. **sojourn**   official visit   swift move   brief stay

11. **iniquities**   sins   qualities   abilities

12. **contentious**   uncouth   argumentative   meddlesome

13. **monosyllabic**   clipped   indifferent   civil

14. **fractious**   domineering   irritable   nosy

15. **disapprobation**   disbelief   discomfort   disfavor

Word Map

auspicious	abominable	magisterial	pestilence
cordiality	benevolence	inquisitive	asinine
edification	ramshackle	malignant	pilgrimage
embalming	aberrations	meteorological	

Directions: Complete a word map like the one below for eight of the vocabulary words above.

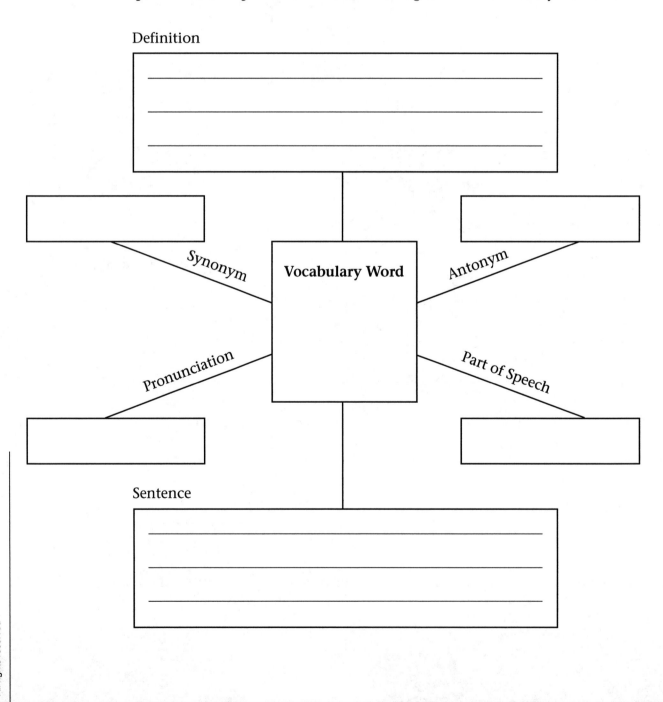

Name _____

Crossword Puzzle

lineaments	ingenuous	changelings	analogous
guilelessness	deportment	obstreperous	invective
mausoleum	erratically	apoplectic	rectitude
interdict	palliation	undulate	propensities

Directions: Select ten vocabulary words from above. Create a crossword puzzle answer key by filling in the grid below. Be sure to number the squares for each word. Blacken any spaces not used by the letters. Then, write clues to the crossword puzzle. Number the clues to match the numbers in the squares. The teacher will give each student a blank grid. Make a blank copy of your crossword puzzle for other students to answer. Exchange your clues with someone else, and solve the blank puzzle s/he gives you. Check the completed puzzles with the answer keys.

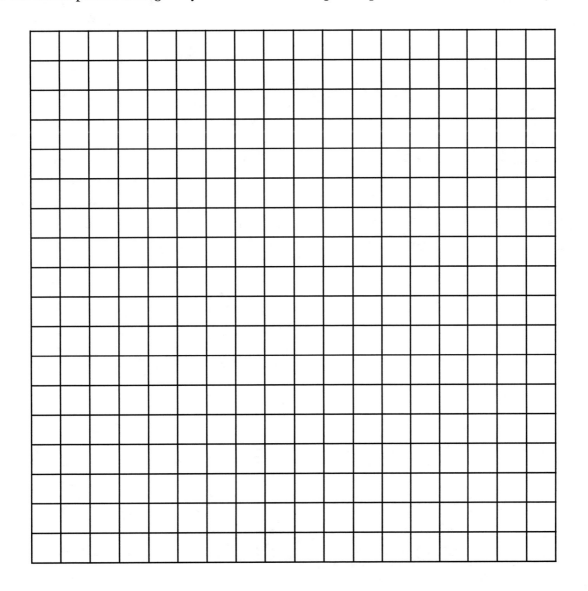

Name _____

Linking Synonyms

altercation	diligently	habiliments	rotogravure
impedimenta	denunciation	prerogative	myopic
penitentiary	resilient	ecclesiastical	succinct
acquiescence	impassive		

Directions: For #1–#3 below, complete each "synonym chain" by adding words that mean the same as the vocabulary word listed. For #4 and #5, create synonym chains for two of the remaining vocabulary words from the list above.

Example:

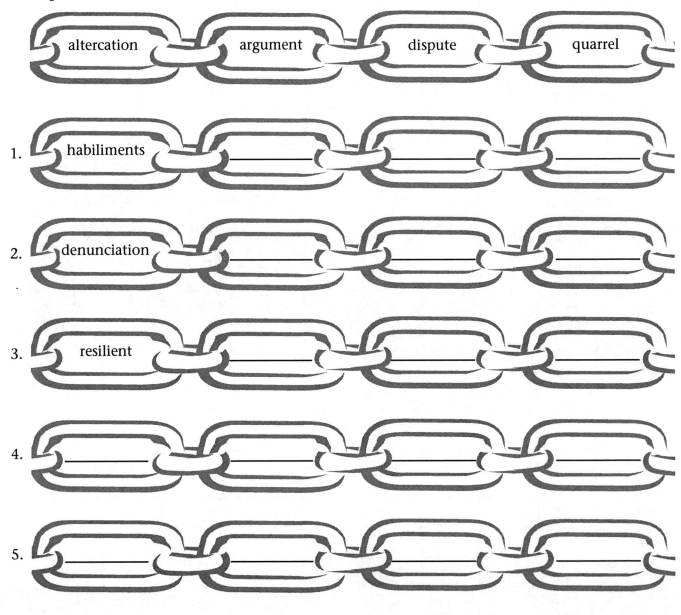

altercation — argument — dispute — quarrel

1. habiliments — _____ — _____ — _____

2. denunciation — _____ — _____ — _____

3. resilient — _____ — _____ — _____

4. _____ — _____ — _____ — _____

5. _____ — _____ — _____ — _____

© Novel Units, Inc.

Name _____

Vocabulary by Association

akimbo	elucidate	unobtrusive	congenital
acrimonious	quelling	tenet	ambidextrous
lavations	mollified	volition	iota
contraband	unmitigated	temerity	caliber

Directions: Define and associate eight of the vocabulary words above with a character from the novel, and in the chart below, explain why each word matches your chosen character's personality. You may associate more than one word with a character, but use no more than three words per character.

Word(s)	Character	Explanation

Vocabulary Analogies

feral	fatalistic	adamant	stolidly
vehement	sordid	wrathfully	duress
largo	replenishing	sibilant	brevity
undelectable	demise	spurious	enunciated

Directions: Complete the analogies below using vocabulary words from the box above. Then, write three analogies of your own using the remaining words.

1. SUBSTANTIAL is to CONSIDERABLE as _____ is to WRETCHED.

2. GENUINE is to TRUE as _____ is to FALSE.

3. GRADUALLY is to LEISURELY as EMOTIONLESSLY is to _____.

4. REFILLING is to _____ as SALVAGING is to REUSING.

5. ACCOMODATING is to _____ as REASSURING is to ANXIOUS.

6. DOMESTIC is to TAME as _____ is to WILD.

7. MUMBLED is to _____ as WHISPERED is to BELLOWED.

8. _____ is to PHILOSOPHY as OPTIMISTIC is to HOPE.

9. PRESSURE is to _____ as CONCERN is to UNEASINESS.

10. STAMMER is to FALTERING as HISS is to _____.

11. _____ is to RAGE as BLISSFULLY is to DELIGHT.

12. NUANCE is to SUBTLE as _____ is to DIGNIFIED.

13. _____ is to APPEALING as IRRESOLUTE is to FIRM.

14. _____ is to _____ as _____ is to

_____.

15. _____ is to _____ as _____ is to

_____.

16. _____ is to _____ as _____ is to

_____.

Name _____

Vocabulary Connections & Summary

annals	florid	carcass	burgle
purloined	contraption	irascible	lectern
ascertain	primeval	pinioned	staccato
untrammeled	perforated	connived	raling

A. Directions: Explain how each pair of words below is related.

1. annals/primeval _____

_____

_____

2. burgle/purloined _____

_____

_____

3. pinioned/untrammeled _____

_____

_____

B. Directions: Write a brief summary of one chapter from this section (Chapters 27–31) using four of the remaining vocabulary words from the list above.

_____

_____

_____

_____

_____

_____

_____

_____

_____

Name _____

Directions: Answer the following questions on a separate sheet of paper. Use your answers in class discussions, for writing assignments, and to review for tests.

Part One
Chapters 1–3

1. How does Scout describe Maycomb, Alabama?
2. What role does Calpurnia play in the Finch household?
3. Why does Jem begin to respect Dill shortly after meeting him?
4. Why hasn't the younger Radley boy been seen in the last 15 years?
5. What does Dill dare Jem to do?
6. Why is Scout reprimanded by Miss Caroline?
7. Why are Scout and Jem surprised by Walter Cunningham's conversation with Atticus?
8. Why does Calpurnia scold Scout while Walter Cunningham is there?
9. What does Miss Caroline see that terrifies her?
10. How does Atticus describe the Ewells?

Chapters 4–8

1. What does Scout find in a knot-hole in a tree near the Radley property?
2. What happens to Scout when she rolls in the tire?
3. What does Scout reveal she heard while she was on the Radley property?
4. How do Scout, Jem, and Dill play "Boo Radley"?
5. Why does Scout begin spending more time with Miss Maudie Atkinson?
6. How do Jem and Dill plan to give Boo Radley a note?
7. How do Scout, Jem, and Dill almost get killed in the Radleys' collard patch?
8. What do Scout and Jem find in the knot-hole that frightens Scout?
9. What is Scout and Jem's "biggest prize"?
10. Why do Scout and Jem eventually stop checking the knot-hole?
11. Why does Scout holler, "The world's endin', Atticus" (p. 86)?
12. Who put a blanket around Scout's shoulders during the fire at Miss Maudie's?

Chapters 9–11

1. Why does Atticus warn Scout that she might hear some "ugly talk" at school?
2. Why does Scout accuse Uncle Jack of not being fair?
3. What advice does Atticus give his brother about avoiding children's questions?

4. What qualities about Atticus make Scout consider him old and feeble?

5. Who is Tim Johnson, and why is he considered dangerous?

6. What changes Scout's and Jem's opinion of their father?

7. Why does Jem destroy Mrs. Dubose's camellia bushes?

8. What is Jem's punishment for this offense?

9. What does Scout realize about her and Jem's reading sessions with Mrs. Dubose?

10. What secret do Scout and Jem learn about Mrs. Dubose after her death?

Part Two
Chapters 12–15

1. Why doesn't Dill visit Maycomb the next summer?

2. Why do Jem and Scout go to church with Calpurnia?

3. How are Scout and Jem treated at First Purchase M.E. Church?

4. Why has Aunt Alexandra come to stay with the Finches?

5. What is Aunt Alexandra's main preoccupation?

6. What triggers an argument about Calpurnia between Atticus and Aunt Alexandra?

7. What do Scout and Jem find under Scout's bed?

8. What is Dill's concern about his mother and stepfather?

9. Why do men assemble in the Finches' yard one evening?

10. How does Scout help disperse the mob surrounding Atticus at the Maycomb jail?

Chapters 16–21

1. How does Atticus defend Mr. Cunningham to his children?

2. Describe the environment at the Maycomb County courthouse on the day of the trial.

3. Where do Scout and Jem sit in the courthouse?

4. What information does Sheriff Tate give on the witness stand?

5. What is the first thing Atticus questions Bob Ewell about on the witness stand?

6. Why does Mayella Ewell think Atticus is mocking her?

7. What do Scout and Jem realize about Tom Robinson when he stands up in court?

8. Why did Tom originally stop at the Ewell residence?

9. What does Tom say that makes Mr. Gilmer nearly "rise to the ceiling" (p. 264)?

10. What do Scout and Dill discover about Dolphus Raymond?

11. What message does Calpurnia bring Atticus?

12. What makes Scout think back to the morning her father shot the rabid dog?

13. What is the jury's verdict?

14. What do people in the Colored balcony do as Atticus passes? Why?

Chapters 22–26

1. What does Calpurnia show the Finches in the kitchen the morning after the trial?

2. What does Miss Maudie call a "baby step"?

3. How does Atticus explain why Maycomb citizens do not serve on juries?

4. Why won't Aunt Alexandra permit Scout to invite Walter over?

5. Why does Aunt Alexandra want Scout to mingle with the ladies at the missionary circle gathering?

6. How does Mrs. Merriweather treat children?

7. Why does Atticus interrupt the missionary circle gathering?

8. Why does Scout begin to respect Aunt Alexandra?

9. How does Dill describe Helen Robinson's reaction to news of her husband's death?

10. Why does Scout question Miss Gates' hatred of Adolf Hitler?

Chapters 27–31

1. What three "small things out of the ordinary" (p. 332) happened in Maycomb between the time of the trial and mid-October?

2. What legendary prank was pulled on Misses Tutti and Frutti Barber?

3. What is Scout's part in the Halloween pageant?

4. Who frightens Scout and Jem on their way to the pageant?

5. How does Scout "ruin" Mrs. Merriweather's pageant?

6. What happens to Scout and Jem on their way home from the pageant?

7. What does Sheriff Tate find under the big oak tree?

8. How does Scout recognize her rescuer as Boo Radley?

9. Why doesn't Sheriff Tate want the public to know the truth?

10. What does Scout do as she stands on Boo Radley's porch?

Name _____

Character Web

Directions: Complete the attribute web below by filling in information specific to Scout.

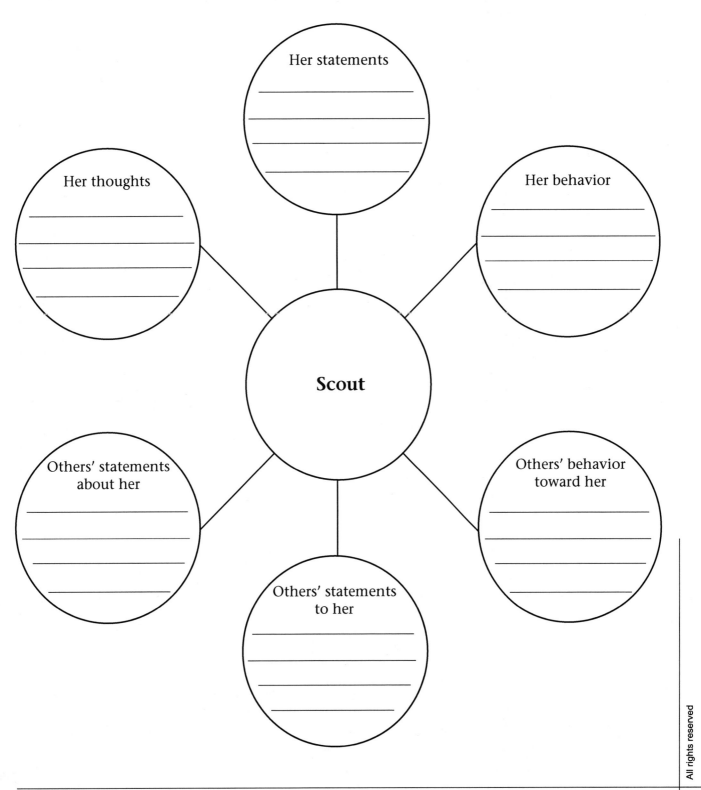

Name _____

Character Chart

Directions: In the boxes across from each of the feelings, describe an incident or time in the novel when each of the listed characters experienced that feeling. You may use "not applicable" if you cannot find an example.

	Scout	Jem	Atticus
Frustration			
Anger			
Fear			
Humiliation			
Relief			
Triumph			

Name _____

The Value of Setting

Directions: A novel's setting contributes to the mood or feeling of the story and often also encompasses the surrounding social environment. In the second column of the chart below, describe each setting listed. In the third column, tell what dramatic value the setting adds to the story.

Setting	Description	Dramatic Value Added
the Radley house		
Miss Caroline's first-grade classroom		
First Purchase African M.E. Church		
Mrs. Dubose's house		
the Maycomb County jailhouse		
the Maycomb County courthouse		

Name _____

Venn Diagram

A. Directions: Using the Venn diagram below, compare and contrast Miss Maudie and Mrs. Dubose.

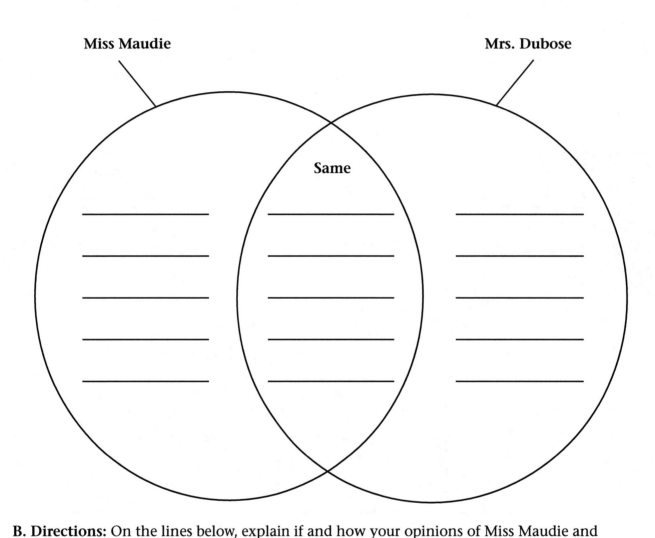

Miss Maudie   Mrs. Dubose

Same

B. Directions: On the lines below, explain if and how your opinions of Miss Maudie and Mrs. Dubose changed as you read the novel.

_____

_____

_____

_____

_____

_____

Cause/Effect Chart

Directions: Make a flow chart to show decisions a character made, the decisions s/he could have made, and the result(s) of each. (Use your imagination to speculate on the results of decisions the character could have made.)

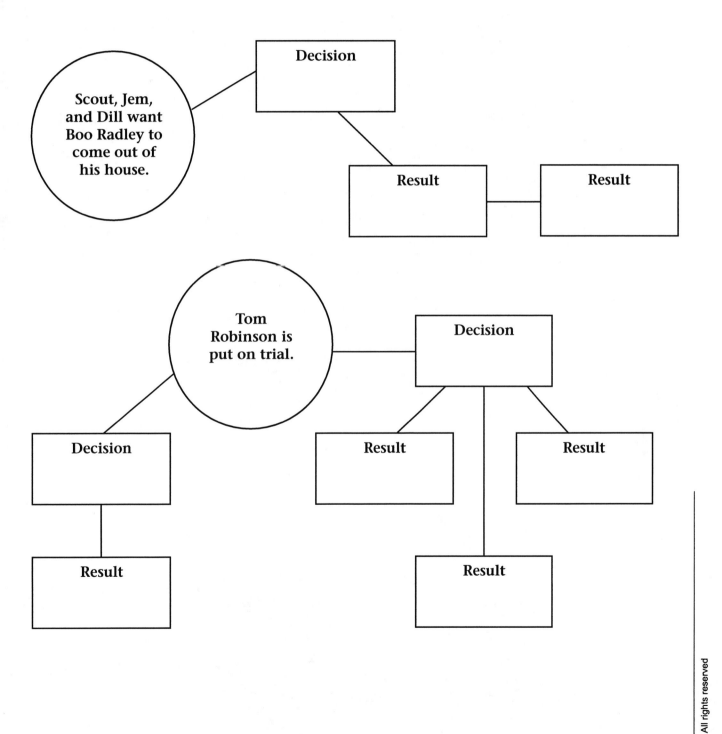

Name _____

Sociogram

Directions: A sociogram shows the relationship between characters in a story. Complete the sociogram below by writing a word to describe the relationships between the characters. Remember, relationships go both ways, so each line requires a descriptive word.

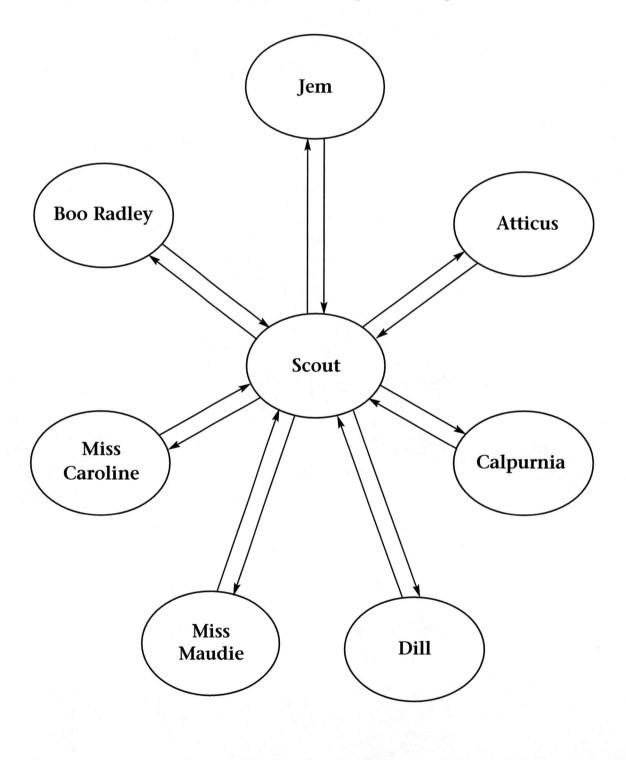

Effects of Reading

Directions: Think about how parts of the novel affected you in different ways. Did some parts make you laugh? cry? want to do something to help someone? Below, list one part of the novel that touched each of the following parts of the body: your head (made you think), your heart (made you feel), your funny bone (made you laugh), or your feet (spurred you to action).

Your head	Your heart

Your funny bone	Your feet

Name _____

Motifs

Directions: A **motif** is an idea that is frequently repeated to underscore an important "life's truth" in a story. In the chart below, describe scenes or incidents from *To Kill a Mockingbird* in which the following motifs appear. Then, state the "life's truth" that is revealed by the use of that motif.

Motif	Scene/Incident	Life's Truth Revealed
heredity/background		
walking in someone else's shoes		
mockingbird		

Story Map

Directions: Fill in each box below with information about the novel.

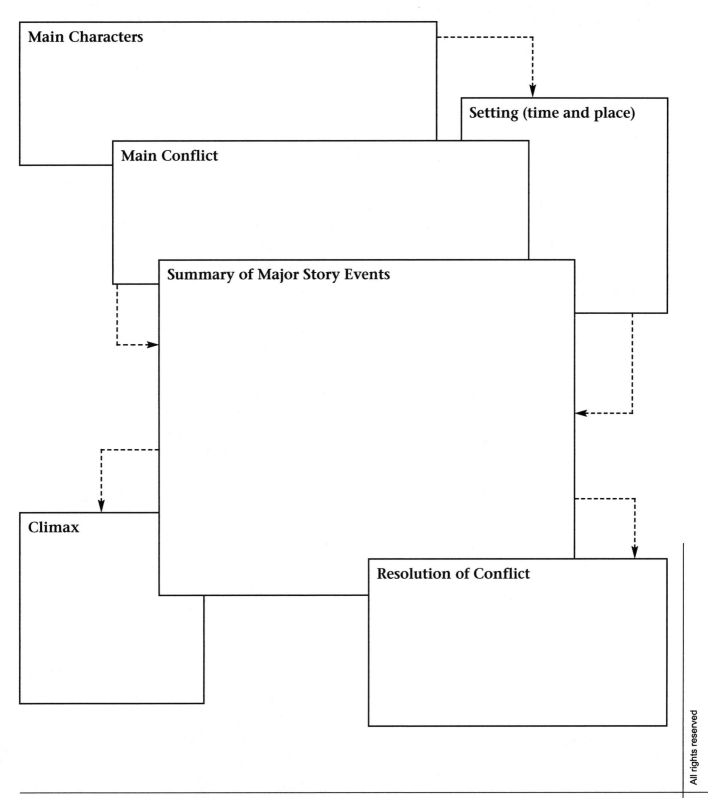

Main Characters

Setting (time and place)

Main Conflict

Summary of Major Story Events

Climax

Resolution of Conflict

Rate This Novel

Directions: How would you rate this novel? How clear were its ideas and characters? Use the scale below to respond to each item. Discuss your answers with the class.

1 ———— 2 ———— 3 ———— 4 ———— 5 ———— 6
very clear   very unclear

Rating

1. description of the setting _____

2. setting's importance _____

3. main character's goal _____

4. main character's problem (why s/he cannot reach the goal) _____

5. main character's plan to solve the problem _____

6. main character's thoughts _____

7. description of secondary characters _____

8. small details of the story _____

9. resolution of the problem at the end of the novel _____

10. novel's main message _____

Name _____

(Character Analysis)

A. Matching: Match each character on the left with the correct description on the right.

____ 1. Scout Finch

____ 2. Jem Finch

____ 3. Atticus Finch

____ 4. Dill Harris

____ 5. Calpurnia

____ 6. Boo Radley

____ 7. Maudie Atkinson

____ 8. Caroline Fisher

____ 9. Walter Cunningham

____ 10. Uncle Jack Finch

a. lawyer; keeps an office that is simple and nearly bare

b. takes great pride in growing and tending azaleas

c. has white "duckfluff" hair; tells wild stories

d. is punished by the teacher on the first day of school

e. cooks for a living; runs a strict household

f. doctor; doesn't understand children

g. knowledgeable about farming; comes from a poor but honest family

h. naïve; easily upset; not accustomed to "country ways"

i. has been forced to stay indoors for years

j. speaks with authority; boastful; a natural leader

(Summarize Major Ideas)

B. Short Answer: Explain how each of the following word(s) is important to the story's plot.

11. syrup

_____

_____

12. knot-hole

_____

_____

13. snowman

_____

_____

14. mad dog

_____

_____

(Cause/Effect)
A. Cause/Effect: Fill in the missing cause or effect for each item below.

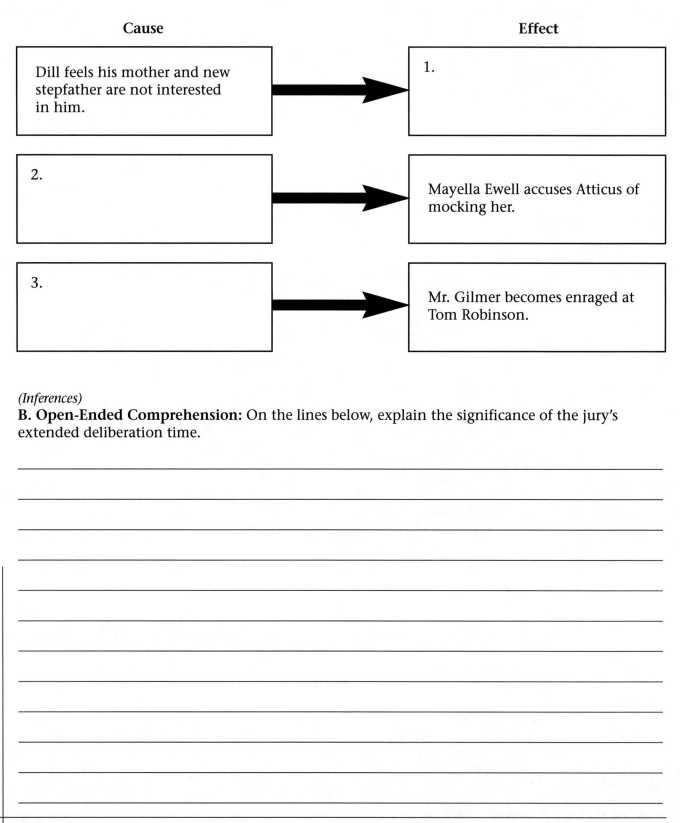

Cause		Effect
Dill feels his mother and new stepfather are not interested in him.	→	1.
2.	→	Mayella Ewell accuses Atticus of mocking her.
3.	→	Mr. Gilmer becomes enraged at Tom Robinson.

(Inferences)
B. Open-Ended Comprehension: On the lines below, explain the significance of the jury's extended deliberation time.

_____

_____

_____

_____

_____

_____

_____

_____

_____

_____

_____

_____

Name _____

(Sequencing)

A. Sequencing: Place the following events in the correct order using the letters *a–j*.

____ 1. Aunt Alexandra forbids Scout from inviting Walter Cunningham over.

____ 2. Scout misses her cue in the Halloween pageant.

____ 3. Atticus reports that Tom Robinson has been killed in an attempted prison escape.

____ 4. Scout sees Boo Radley for the first time.

____ 5. Atticus reads *The Gray Ghost* aloud to Scout.

____ 6. Scout questions Miss Gates' hypocrisy.

____ 7. Link Deas warns Bob Ewell against harassing Helen Robinson.

____ 8. Bob Ewell spits in Atticus's face and tells him he will "get him."

____ 9. Scout and Jem are attacked in the dark.

____ 10. Mrs. Merriweather refers to Atticus as "good but misguided."

(Compare/Contrast)

B. Open-Ended Comprehension: Compare Stoner's Boy (from *The Gray Ghost*) to Boo Radley.

_____

_____

_____

_____

_____

_____

_____

_____

_____

_____

_____

_____

_____

_____

(Main Idea and Details)
A. True/False: Mark each with a *T* for true or an *F* for false. Correct any false statements on the line provided.

_____ 1. Jem begins to respect Dill because Dill has seen *Dracula*.

_____

_____ 2. Scout rubs Walter Cunningham's nose in the dirt because he stole her lunch.

_____

_____ 3. Scout, Jem, and Dill entertain themselves by playing a game based on Boo Radley legends.

_____

_____ 4. Miss Rachel Haverford's house burns down.

_____

_____ 5. Uncle Jack forgives Francis for his negative comments about Atticus.

_____

_____ 6. Scout and Jem go to church with Calpurnia because Calpurnia doesn't trust them to go to their church alone.

_____

_____ 7. Aunt Alexandra forbids Scout from visiting Calpurnia's home.

_____

_____ 8. Miss Stephanie Crawford refuses to attend Tom Robinson's trial.

_____

_____ 9. Tom's left arm was crippled in a cotton gin accident.

_____

_____ 10. Mrs. Merriweather claims Scout ruined the school pageant.

_____

(Character Analysis)
B. Quotations: Match each character to the correct quote.

____ 11. "Your father does not know how to teach. You can have a seat now."

____ 12. "...I'm not much of a drinker, but you see they could never, never understand that I live like I do because that's the way I want to live."

____ 13. "...I can use one hand good as the other. One hand good as the other...."

____ 14. "...there's just some kind of men you have to shoot before you can say hidy to 'em."

____ 15. "I felt right sorry for her, she seemed to try more'n the rest of 'em—"

____ 16. "The world's endin'.... Please do something—!"

____ 17. "Forgot to tell you the other day that besides playing the Jew's Harp, Atticus Finch was the deadest shot in Maycomb County in his time."

____ 18. "My paw's never touched a hair o'my head in my life...."

____ 19. "...before I can live with other folks I've got to live with myself. The one thing that doesn't abide by majority rule is a person's conscience."

____ 20. "Now I mean it...you antagonize Aunty and I'll—I'll spank you."

a. Scout
b. Jem
c. Atticus
d. Miss Maudie
e. Miss Caroline
f. Sheriff Tate
g. Dolphus Raymond
h. Tom Robinson
i. Bob Ewell
j. Mayella Ewell

C. Multiple Choice: Choose the BEST answer.

(Main Idea and Details)
____ 21. Who originates the idea of making Boo Radley come out of his house?
   a. Dill
   b. Francis
   c. Jem
   d. Scout

(Character Analysis)
____ 22. Miss Caroline could best be described as
   a. seasoned and strict
   b. gentle and accepting
   c. naïve and easily rattled
   d. jaded and overly cynical

(Inferences)
____ 23. Why does Atticus want Scout and Jem to alter their snowman?
   a. He thinks Mr. Avery might be offended by the likeness.
   b. He doesn't want his children taking snow from neighbors' yards.
   c. He doesn't want to give people more reason to focus on the Finch home.
   d. He thinks Miss Maudie would find humor in a snowman that resembled her.

(Drawing Conclusions)
____ 24. How does Scout effectively disperse a mob gathered at the Maycomb jailhouse one night?
   a. Her endless chatter tires the men gathered.
   b. Her presence makes the mob reluctant to harm her father.
   c. Her courtesy and childhood innocence touch those assembled.
   d. Her knowledge of legal matters makes the men forget their original intent.

(Inferences)
____ 25. Why do the people sitting in the Colored balcony rise as Atticus passes?
   a. to protest the guilty verdict
   b. as a symbol of respect for Atticus
   c. to hide Scout and Jem in the crowd
   d. as a show of support for Helen Robinson

(Summarize Major Ideas)
D. Identification: Explain how each of the following words or phrases is important to the story.

26. "One Man's Family"

_____

_____

_____

27. morphine

_____

_____

_____

28. entailment

_____

_____

_____

29. knife

_____

_____

_____

30. *The Gray Ghost*

_____

_____

_____

E. Essay: Respond to three of the following in well-developed essays. Cite evidence from the novel to support your responses.

(Literary Devices)
  I. How is a mockingbird used as a metaphor throughout the novel?

(Summarize Major Ideas/Character Analysis)
  II. How does Atticus raise his children somewhat unconventionally? Discuss whether you think Atticus is a good father and why.

(Point of View)
  III. What impact does Scout's point of view give the story? Explain.

(Theme)
  IV. Find and discuss an example of each of the following themes in the novel: hypocrisy, injustice, prejudice.

(Interpret Text)
  V. Discuss the possible meaning(s) of Atticus's statement: "Most people are [really nice], Scout, when you finally see them" (p. 376).

Answer Key

Activities #1–#2: Answers will vary.

Activity #3: 1. relieved 2. statement 3. reserved 4. unspoiled 5. bland 6. wicked 7. preference 8. vague 9. native 10. brief stay 11. sins 12. argumentative 13. clipped 14. irritable 15. disfavor

Activity #4: Word maps will vary. Example—Vocabulary Word: auspicious; Definition: marked by success; Synonym: promising; Antonym: ill-fated; Pronunciation: aw-**spish**-uhs; Part of Speech: adjective; Sentence: The ceremony evolved from an *auspicious* celebration of achievement to a boring, drawn-out event.

Activity #5: Crossword puzzles will vary.

Activity #6: Synonym chains will vary. Suggestions—1. apparel, clothing, garb 2. indictment, reprehension, condemnation 3. supple, pliable, rubbery

Activity #7: Associations will vary. Example—Word: caliber; Character: Atticus; Explanation: The high *caliber* of Atticus's character is well-known in Maycomb.

Activity #8: 1. sordid 2. spurious 3. stolidly 4. replenishing 5. adamant 6. feral 7. enunciated 8. fatalistic 9. duress 10. sibilant 11. wrathfully 12. largo 13. undelectable 14.–16. Analogies will vary.

Activity #9: A. Connections will vary. Suggestions—1. The words *annals* and *primeval* both relate to the past. 2. The words *burgle* and *purloined* both relate to stealing. 3. The words *pinioned* and *untrammeled* both relate to restraint. **B.** Summaries will vary.

Study Guide
Part One
Chapters 1–3: 1. as a tired, slow-paced old town with unpaved streets which gets very hot in the summer 2. Calpurnia is the Finches' cook and surrogate mother. 3. Dill has seen the movie *Dracula*. 4. He fell in with the wrong crowd and was charged with "disorderly conduct, disturbing the peace, assault and battery, and using abusive and profane language in the presence and hearing of a female" (p. 12). In lieu of having his son sent to the industrial school, Mr. Radley forced his son to become a shut-in. 5. touch Boo Radley's house 6. because she already knows how to read and because she unwittingly embarrasses Miss Caroline by attempting to explain the Cunninghams' financial situation 7. because Walter and Atticus carry on an adult conversation about farming 8. because Scout disgraces her family by ridiculing Walter, the Finches' "company," at the dinner table 9. lice crawling on Burris Ewell's head 10. as a family whose members had never done an honest day's work, lived "like animals," and were generally "the disgrace of Maycomb" (p. 40)

Chapters 4–8: 1. two pieces of unwrapped chewing gum 2. The tire rolls out of control, depositing Scout on the Radley property. 3. someone laughing inside the house 4. The children use bits of neighborhood legend and gossip to concoct wild stories about the Radleys, which they then act out. 5. Dill and Jem become closer and begin excluding Scout because she is a girl. 6. by using a fishing pole to pass the note through the Radleys' shutters 7. They are trying to peek into the house at Boo Radley, but Nathan Radley believes someone is trespassing on his property and fires his shotgun. 8. two soap miniatures that resemble Scout and Jem 9. a broken pocket watch 10. Nathan Radley fills it with cement. 11. It snows in Maycomb, and Scout has never seen snow before. 12. Boo Radley

Chapters 9–11: 1. because Atticus is defending a black man named Tom Robinson in an upcoming trial and many townspeople don't believe he should 2. Uncle Jack does not allow Scout to explain why she was fighting with Francis; instead, he immediately assumes Scout is the only one who did something wrong. 3. Atticus tells Jack to answer children's questions truthfully because children "can spot an evasion quicker than adults, and evasion simply muddles 'em" (p. 116). 4. Atticus is older than their classmates' parents, refuses to play tackle football, works in an office, wears glasses, and does not hunt, play poker, fish, drink, or smoke. 5. Harry Johnson's dog and "the pet of Maycomb" (p. 122); The dog appears to be rabid. 6. Scout and Jem discover that Atticus is "the deadest shot in Maycomb County" (p. 129), though he has never bragged about his talent. 7. Mrs. Dubose makes harsh comments about Atticus. 8. He must read to Mrs. Dubose every day after school and on Saturdays for a month. 9. The sessions last longer each day. 10. Mrs. Dubose was a morphine addict, and the children's presence helped her beat her addiction before she died.

Part Two

Chapters 12–15: 1. Dill is building a fishing boat with his new stepfather in Meridian. 2. Atticus did not give Calpurnia specific directions about the children attending church when he left, and Calpurnia is afraid they will misbehave if they go alone. 3. They are welcomed by most of the congregation except a woman named Lula, who claims Scout and Jem have "no business" at First Purchase. 4. to expose Scout to some "feminine influence" 5. heredity or "background" 6. Scout reporting that she and Jem went to First Purchase and expressing desire to visit Calpurnia's home 7. Dill 8. that they are not interested in him 9. to warn Atticus about potential difficulties and danger regarding the Tom Robinson case 10. Scout makes friendly conversation with Mr. Cunningham, unwittingly making him feel ashamed of his actions.

Chapters 16–21: 1. Atticus claims Mr. Cunningham is "basically a good man [but] just has his blind spots" (p. 210). 2. Scout describes it as a "gala occasion," with "no room at the public hitching rail for another animal" (p. 214). People eat and socialize on the lawn before the trial. 3. in the Colored balcony 4. He describes how Bob Ewell called him claiming that a black man had raped his daughter, Mayella. Mayella named Tom Robinson as her attacker. Sheriff Tate also describes Mayella's specific injuries. 5. whether Bob ran for a doctor once he realized Mayella had been assaulted 6. Atticus calls her "ma'am" and "Miss Mayella"—courtesies she is unaccustomed to and interprets as disrespect. 7. His left arm is crippled, making it impossible for him to have inflicted the injuries the Ewells claim he did. 8. Mayella asked him to chop up an old piece of furniture. 9. Tom says he felt sorry for Mayella. 10. He is not really a drunk; he merely pretends to be so people find it easier to accept his lifestyle. 11. a message from Aunt Alexandra that Scout and Jem are missing 12. the anticipatory atmosphere in the courtroom 13. They unanimously vote "guilty." 14. stand up; as a show of respect

Chapters 22–26: 1. a variety of food that was sent by Maycomb's grateful black community 2. the jury deliberating for as long as they did 3. He says they are both uninterested in and afraid of the responsibility of being jurors. 4. Aunt Alexandra believes the Cunninghams are too low-class for Scout to associate with. 5. It is "part of her campaign to teach [Scout] to be a lady" (p. 307). 6. condescendingly, as if they do not understand adult matters 7. Tom has been killed, and he wants Calpurnia to help him tell Tom's wife. 8. Scout admires how Aunt Alexandra keeps her composure during a crisis. 9. "...she just fell down in the dirt...like a giant with a big foot just came along and stepped on her" (p. 322). 10. Scout cannot understand how Miss Gates can be so sensitive to some types of prejudice and numb to others (e.g., racial prejudice in Maycomb).

Chapters 27–31: 1. Bob Ewell got and lost a job with the WPA, an attempted burglary took place at Judge Taylor's house, and Link Deas hired Helen Robinson. 2. Mischievous Maycomb children removed the furniture from their livingroom and placed it in their basement. 3. a ham 4. Cecil Jacobs 5. Scout misses her cue and embarrasses Mrs. Merriweather by appearing onstage as Mrs. Merriweather marches on waving the state flag. 6. Someone follows and attacks them in the dark. 7. Bob Ewell's dead body 8. She suddenly notices his sickly pallor and timid demeanor. 9. because then Boo Radley would be placed in the limelight, which Sheriff Tate believes would be cruel 10. Scout imagines everyday scenes as Boo would see them.

Note: Answers to Activities #10–#19 will vary. Suggested responses are given where applicable.

Activity #10: Examples—Her thoughts: "[Jem's] maddening superiority was unbearable..." (p. 184); Her statements: "You [Atticus] never went to school and you do all right, so I'll just stay home too" (p. 39); Her behavior: "This time, I split my knuckle to the bone on [Francis's] front teeth" (p. 112); Others' behavior toward her: "...Atticus doesn't ever just listen to Jem's side of it, he hears mine too..." (p. 113); Others' statements to her: "It's time you started bein' a girl and acting right!" (p. 153); Others' statements about her: "...[Scout] minds me as well as she can. Doesn't come up to scratch half the time, but she tries" (p. 116).

Activity #11: Example for Jem—Frustration: when the "guilty" verdict is announced at the end of Tom Robinson's trial; Anger: when Scout recounts what she overheard Miss Gates saying outside the courthouse; Fear: when Jem sees a shadowy figure on the Radleys' back porch; Humiliation: when Jem appears in public with no pants after they get caught on the Radleys' fence; Relief: when Jem is able to leave Mrs. Dubose's house after reading to her each day; Triumph: when Jem hears Atticus's case and thinks his father will win the trial

Activity #12: Example for Mrs. Dubose's house—Description: ominous, dismal, frightening, malodorous; Dramatic Value Added: The house is as decrepit as its owner, creating suspense while Scout and Jem are visiting Mrs. Dubose. Its tomb-like interior subtly foreshadows Mrs. Dubose's death soon after Jem completes his "punishment."

Activity #13: A. Suggestions—Miss Maudie: kind to Scout and Jem, enjoys gardening, resistant to bandwagon mentality; Mrs. Dubose: mean to Scout and Jem, addicted to morphine for most of her life, prejudiced about race and class; Same: blunt and outspoken, concerned with propriety and manners, wise, respects Atticus **B.** Answers will vary.

Activity #14: Examples—(Top chart) Decision: The three children decide they will attempt to peer into the Radley house; Result: The children are almost injured; Result: Jem loses his pants on the fence; (Bottom chart) Decision: Tom Robinson is found guilty; Result: Tom is killed when trying to escape from prison; Decision: Bob Ewell decides he must get revenge on Atticus for making him look foolish in court; Result: Bob Ewell threatens Atticus publicly; Result: Bob Ewell attempts to kill Scout and Jem; Result: Bob Ewell is killed by Boo Radley.

Activity #15: Suggestions—Scout to Jem: admiring; Jem to Scout: authoritative; Scout to Atticus: inquisitive; Atticus to Scout: patient; Scout to Calpurnia: exasperating; Calpurnia to Scout: firm; Scout to Dill: accepting; Dill to Scout: boastful; Scout to Miss Maudie: interested; Miss Maudie to Scout: straightforward; Scout to Miss Caroline: informative; Miss Caroline to Scout: vexed; Scout to Boo Radley: fascinated; Boo Radley to Scout: protective

Activity #16: Answers will vary.

Activity #17: Examples—Motif: heredity/background; Scene/Incident: Scout vows to invite Walter Cunningham to the Finch home, but Aunt Alexandra forbids it; Life's Truth Revealed: Heredity/background simply breeds ignorance and a false sense of superiority. A person's true character is revealed by his or her words and deeds; Motif: walking in someone else's shoes; Scene/Incident: Scout pauses on Boo Radley's porch at the end of the novel to gain some perspective on his life; Life's Truth Revealed: Some people cannot cope with the hatefulness and danger in the world but take pleasure from small things; Motif: mockingbird; Scene/Incident: Scout realizes exposing Boo Radley to public scrutiny and judgment would be like shooting a harmless, inoffensive bird like the mockingbird; Life's Truth Revealed: Persecuting harmless, defenseless beings is a terrible sin to commit.

Activity #18: Suggestions—Main Characters: Scout, Jem, Atticus, Aunt Alexandra, Calpurnia, Dill, the Radleys, the Ewells, Miss Maudie, Tom Robinson; Setting: 1930s in the small Southern town of Maycomb, Alabama; Main Conflict: A black man, Tom Robinson, is on trial for the rape of a white woman, Mayella Ewell, in a place and time when racial prejudice runs rampant; Summary of Major Story Events: Scout Finch recalls her childhood in Maycomb, describing the mischievous deeds she, her brother, and their neighbor's nephew Dill commit. One summer, Scout is forced to realize that hate and ignorance exist in the world when Tom Robinson is convicted of a crime he obviously did not commit; Climax: As a result of their father's involvement with the trial, Scout and Jem are almost killed one night by Bob Ewell, the father of the plaintiff in the Tom Robinson case; Resolution of Conflict: The Finches' reclusive neighbor Boo Radley rescues Scout and Jem.

Activity #19: Answers will vary.

Quiz #1: A. 1. d 2. j 3. a 4. c 5. e 6. i 7. b 8. h 9. g 10. f **B.** Answers will vary. Suggestions—11. When Walter douses his food in *syrup*, Scout is quick to criticize him, earning herself a chiding from Calpurnia about being courteous to company. 12. Scout and Jem begin finding small "treasures" in the *knot-hole* of a live oak near the Radley property, leading them to wonder who is leaving the treats (and become even more curious about the Radley family). 13. Scout and Jem build a *snowman* that bears a striking resemblance to the round Mr. Avery, providing a humorous moment in the story. 14. When a *mad dog* enters their neighborhood, Scout and Jem witness their father's shooting prowess firsthand, gaining Atticus new respect from his children.

Quiz #2: A. 1. Effect—Dill runs away to Maycomb, where he hides under Scout's bed until he is discovered. 2. Cause—Atticus calls Mayella "ma'am" and "Miss Mayella," and she is unaccustomed to this courtesy. 3. Cause—Tom Robinson says he helped Mayella Ewell because he felt sorry for her. **B.** Answers will vary. Though Atticus defended Tom excellently, everyone knows that the case will ultimately boil down to race. The fact that the jury did not return immediately is unusual, as a white man's word is normally automatically believed over a black man's. The extended deliberation time is a "baby step" toward progress in racial equality.

Quiz #3: A. 1. b 2. g 3. d 4. i 5. j 6. e 7. f 8. a 9. h 10. c (p. 311) **B.** Answers will vary. Like Stoner's Boy, Boo Radley is suspected of committing heinous deeds. As a shadowy, frightening figure that exists mostly in Maycomb children's imaginations, Boo Radley is "stalked" (like Stoner's Boy is persecuted) by Scout, Jem, and Dill, whose only wish is to glimpse this elusive figure. Scout says of the Stoner's Boy: "…when they finally saw him, why he hadn't done any of those things…he was real nice…" (p. 376). Similarly, when Scout finally meets Boo Radley, he is timid yet friendly—the contrary to what she had always believed.

Novel Test: A. 1. T 2. F; Scout rubs his nose in the dirt because she believes he is to blame for her getting into trouble with Miss Caroline. 3. T 4. F; Miss Maudie Atkinson's house burns down. 5. F; Uncle Jack wants to reprimand Francis for what he said about Atticus. 6. T 7. T 8. F; Miss Stephanie Crawford attends the trial, while Miss Maudie refuses to attend. 9. T 10. T **B.** 11. e (p. 23) 12. g (p. 268) 13. i (p. 238) 14. f (p. 361) 15. h (p. 264) 16. a (p. 86) 17. d (p. 129) 18. j (p. 246) 19. c (p. 140) 20. b (p. 184) **C.** 21. a 22. c 23. a 24. c 25. b **D.** Answers will vary. Suggestions—26. "One Man's Family" is the Boo Radley drama that Scout, Jem, and Dill act out to entertain themselves, adding additional outrageous scenes by the day. The children continue playing the game until Atticus realizes what they are doing and orders them to stop. 27. Mrs. Dubose has a morphine addiction—a fact Scout and Jem are unaware of until after Mrs. Dubose's death. By reading to the old woman almost every day, Jem helps her conquer her addiction (by prolonging the intervals between doses). 28. Early in the novel, Scout recalls overhearing a conversation between her father and Mr. Cunningham about Mr. Cunningham's entailment. Later in the novel, when Atticus is facing a mob outside the Maycomb jailhouse, Scout brings up Mr. Cunningham's entailment, reminding him of her father's kindness and generosity. 29. At the end of the novel, Bob Ewell attempts to attack Scout and Jem with a switchblade. However, Boo Radley emerges from his house and kills Bob with a kitchen knife. In the aftermath, Sheriff Tate removes the switchblade from the scene so it will appear that Bob Ewell fell on his own knife—the kitchen knife. 30. *The Gray Ghost* is a novel Dill "swaps" Jem at the beginning of the story after Jem touches the Radley house on a dare. At the end of the story, Atticus reads *The Gray Ghost* aloud to Scout as Jem rests, and the reader is encouraged to draw parallels between Stoner's Boy and Boo Radley. **E.** Essays will vary. Refer to the scoring rubric on page 36 of this guide.

Linking Novel Units® Student Packets to National and State Reading Assessments

During the past several years, an increasing number of students have faced some form of state-mandated competency testing in reading. Many states now administer state-developed assessments to measure the skills and knowledge emphasized in their particular reading curriculum. This Novel Units® guide includes open-ended comprehension questions that correlate with state-mandated reading assessments. The rubric below provides important information for evaluating responses to open-ended comprehension questions. Teachers may also use scoring rubrics provided for their own state's competency test.

Scoring Rubric for Open-Ended Items

3-Exemplary	Thorough, complete ideas/information Clear organization throughout Logical reasoning/conclusions Thorough understanding of reading task Accurate, complete response
2-Sufficient	Many relevant ideas/pieces of information Clear organization throughout most of response Minor problems in logical reasoning/conclusions General understanding of reading task Generally accurate and complete response
1-Partially Sufficient	Minimally relevant ideas/information Obvious gaps in organization Obvious problems in logical reasoning/conclusions Minimal understanding of reading task Inaccuracies/incomplete response
0-Insufficient	Irrelevant ideas/information No coherent organization Major problems in logical reasoning/conclusions Little or no understanding of reading task Generally inaccurate/incomplete response